beginnings

an introduction to Christian faith

Small-Group Leader's Guide

Andy Langford and Mark Ralls

Abingdon Press / Nashville

Beginnings: An Introduction to Christian Faith
Small-Group Leader's Guide

This book is printed on acid-free, elemental chlorine-free paper.

ISBN 0-687-07295-6

03 04 05 06 07 08 09 10 11 12 — 10 9 8 7 6 5 4 3 2

MANUFACTURED IN THE UNITED STATES OF AMERICA

Contents

Introduction

Beginnings: Small-Group Leaders Guide is the resource for small-group discussion leaders in congregations that are offering *Beginnings: An Introduction to Christian Faith.* This resource is used in conjunction with *Beginnings: Director's Manual,* the key organizational resource; *Beginnings: Video Resources,* a set of presentations that introduce a Christian response to basic questions of life; *Beginnings: Participant's Guide,* a workbook for program participants; and *Beginnings: Along the Way: A Participant's Companion,* a book that is the foundation of and expands upon the video presentations.

Part One:

Preparing for *Beginnings*

1.
Welcome to *Beginnings*

Welcome to the twelve sessions of *Beginnings: An Introduction to Christian Faith.* We believe these next few weeks will be among the most important in your life and in the lives of the people you will lead. Each week you will guide a group of inquirers who are asking fundamental questions about life. With your guidance, they will explore who they are, who God is, and how our lives intersect with God. Each week the group members will hear a presentation by Rob Weber about profound questions of human life and how Christians respond to them. Small groups will then gather for discussion led by you and, if your group is larger than ten persons, other members of your leadership team. Each of us is a work in progress, and in these times together you may discover some serious work going on. These few weeks may change the lives of many people, including possibly your own. Together women and men will discover who Christians believe God is, how God touches our lives through Jesus Christ, and how our relationship with God may be strengthened through specific Christian practices such as Bible study, prayer, forgiveness, and service to others.

D. T. Niles, a famous evangelist in the first half of the twentieth century, once described evangelism as "one beggar telling another beggar where to get food."[1] This is the goal of *Beginnings*. This program allows you to share an opening course of the gospel feast, not as an expert with all the answers, but with the humility of one beggar sharing spiritual food with another hungry person. As you share with your group members the basic beliefs and practices of the Christian faith, you invite fellow spiritual beggars on a journey of discovery. This journey encompasses both self-discovery and the growing awareness that each of us has already been discovered by God. Like the sower in Jesus' parable, you will scatter the seeds of the good news of Jesus Christ upon all sorts of ground—some rocky, some thin, some covered with weeds, and some that is fertile. We then leave it to the work of the Holy Spirit to see what will take root and grow (Luke 8:4-8).

Welcome, sower, to the journey!

1. From "Venite Adoremus II," in *World's Student Christian Federation Prayer Book*; pages 105ff.

2.
Small-Group Leaders

The small-group community you lead in *Beginnings: An Introduction to Christian Faith* may be the most important component of this entire program. The small-group discussion, which follows Rob Weber's video/DVD presentation each week, brings all the participants into a relationship with one another; with your congregation; and, most importantly, with Jesus Christ. Just as Jesus chose twelve ordinary people to be his first followers, so Jesus promised that he is present whenever two or three persons are gathered together in his name (Matthew 18:20). You are the host of this Christ-centered gathering.

WHY WERE YOU CHOSEN AS A SMALL-GROUP LEADER?

As a discussion leader, you guide all the participants toward Jesus Christ. In this task you are acting like Jesus' first disciple, Simon Peter. In the Gospel of Mark, the first words of Jesus to Simon the fisherman were, "Follow me and I will make you fish for people" (Mark 1:17). Then, in John's Gospel, Jesus' last words to Simon, now called Peter the Rock, were to "feed" and "tend" the people of God (John 21:15-19). We believe that you, like Simon Peter, have a personal relationship with Jesus Christ and a desire to share your experiences with other people. You truly are the Peter-like companion on the journey for every participant in your small group. We believe that you have the God-given gifts and talents to serve in this role.

PRELIMINARY DETAILS

Your weekly task begins at the start of each session. You are the hospitable host who welcomes each participant, and especially the persons who are in your small group. Over a meal or refreshments, your job is to help people feel welcome by learning their names and listening to their stories. Essentially, you are meeting some new people who may well become your companions in our Christian faith.

After the meal/refreshments and gathering time, everyone watches a video/DVD presentation about a basic question of life. In each session all participants will see and hear Rob Weber talking about a biblical story that helps us understand some part of the Christian life. At the end of the presentation, you will guide the members of your small group in a discussion of the presentation and the questions they have.

Your small group should include between six and twelve people (including you and any helpers you have). Up to one-third of your small group, including you, may be hosts helping with the program.

If there is more than one small group in the program, your director will assign you to a space that your group will occupy each week. At the first few meetings, there will be a sign with your name or group number that identifies your group's space. Your group should sit in a circle or around a table. Everyone should be able to see the face of everyone else clearly and to hear plainly. Encourage people to rotate where they sit so that they will sit next to and meet someone new at each session. At the end of the session, if requested, straighten up the room and put away the chairs and other materials.

You have been designated as the small-group leader. Another person has been designated as your primary assistant, and possibly one or two other persons in your group have been designated as helpers. You and your primary assistant should definitely come to the opening organizational meeting that takes place a few minutes before the sessions begin every week.

If there is more than one small group in the program, your director will assign participants to your small group. We hope that all participants will find other people in your group who are similar to them. No one wants to be the odd person out. Recognize that there is high stress in joining a new group in which most people are strangers. If a person is uncomfortable in your group, he or she probably will not come back. If you discover that someone wishes to move to a different group, talk with your director and make a change by the next meeting without creating a major fuss.

LEADING YOUR SMALL GROUP:
Be Open to the Leading of the Holy Spirit

How do you accompany the participants in your group on this journey, especially those who are not yet active in any community of faith? Your goal as a discussion leader is to enable spiritual growth along God's way by each group member. Your task is to encourage each person to understand and to be open to the grace of God in her or his own life. Even though the group members have heard the same content through the presentation, the basis for your group discussion is not "What did Rob Weber intend to say?" but "What did you hear in this biblical story and presentation that connects to your life or illuminates your experiences?" The questions we provide for each session will assist you with this work, but our experience is that people are eager to talk as soon as the presentation is over. The members of your small group simply need a wise guide to shape their conversation.

In light of this approach, you do not need to provide "correct" answers to questions. Instead, you are to create an environment where possible answers are explored and additional questions may be asked. In response to these presentations, a good discussion is not a debate about any particular person's ideas but a mutual sharing of experiences and opinions. Even though your group members will have heard the same presentation, your group discussions may move in unexpectedly different directions. Do your best to be open to the movement of the Holy Spirit and to be vigilant in discerning the difference between following the Spirit's lead and going off on a side road. Working in partnership with the Holy Spirit, who alone can bring about spiritual transformation, you may achieve marvelous things. Your success as a small-group leader will not be judged by what your group members "know" by the end of this program but by the way their lives are changed in the months and years to come.

In summary, you will read and study each week the material in this SMALL-GROUP LEADER'S GUIDE and the accompanying book, *Beginnings: Along the Way: A Participant's Companion*; watch and listen to the video/DVD presentations along with the participants in your small group; and facilitate your participants in sharing with the group. You may lead by offering your own honest reflections, but you will be even more successful if you enable your group members to listen carefully to one another and to the Holy Spirit. You are the one who leads your participants in a movement from the head to the heart to the hands and feet.

YOUR GIFTS AS A SMALL-GROUP LEADER

Leading small groups requires particular gifts and skills. As you guide the small-group members toward Jesus Christ, you need a variety of God-given gifts, including patience, care, support, encouragement, openness, silence, peace, and prayer. In addition, you should be fully prepared for each session, gently guide the conversation, avoid fixing problems, and watch the clock. When you exhibit these gifts and skills, all the participants can be confident about their guide and companion in the way toward Jesus Christ.

1. Patience is among the qualities that you need most as a discussion leader. Be patient, and let the Holy Spirit guide the process. While you may wish for rapid success, we encourage you to remember that the development of a relationship with Jesus Christ is a lifelong process. It may be difficult to identify any great leap on any particular day, but over time God is at work in the life of every person. Trust the work of the Holy Spirit as you meet with your small group.

2. Care for each person in your small group. Good shepherds watch carefully over each of their sheep. The aim of *Beginnings: An Introduction to Christian Faith* is that every single woman and man should be nurtured, which is why you have multiple congregational hosts in your small group. After the first session, assign one of your small-group hosts to take responsibility for two or three of the participants in your small group. Care can be shown in a number of ways. For example, if one of your participants misses a meeting, it is your responsibility to check and be sure nothing is wrong. Be careful, however, not to be too aggressive in this shepherding. It is appropriate to call participants on the phone or send an e-mail if they miss a session and to express concern and offer appropriate support. If someone was sick, send a get-well card and provide a summary of what happened in the session. If someone did not have transportation, offer to arrange a ride. It is, however, inappropriate to call a participant and berate her or him for missing a session. If someone wants to end the relationship or stop attending the sessions, let him or her go with a prayer. This system of one-on-one care is one of the most crucial aspects of *Beginnings.*

3. Support spiritual growth. While spiritual maturity cannot develop overnight, you can assist your participants through the early stages of their walk and later help integrate them into a congregational group once they have completed *Beginnings.* In general, you should tend to be more active earlier in the program, when people do not know one another well, and then back away as your group matures. Be attuned to the interests of your group members so that once they have completed *Beginnings,* you are prepared to guide them to other experiences within your congregation. If participants within your group who are not members of your congregation start attending worship services in your church, arrange to meet and sit with them. Also encourage them to become involved in various congregational activities.

Part of encouraging spiritual maturity is to help participants avoid attaching themselves to any leader other than Jesus Christ. For example, good parents begin by feeding their children; but as the children grow, mature parents teach their children to feed themselves. Beware of any unhealthy dependence by any of your participants upon any leader. Instead, encourage your group members to grow in their relationships with a variety of people within the weekly gatherings and maybe within your congregation. Your small group is the ideal place to start developing such friendships.

4. Encourage. In the early church, Barnabas and the apostles encouraged Paul. In response, Paul urged new Christians to "encourage one another and build up each other" (1 Thessalonians 5:11). In our modern society, negative criticism dominates our political and cultural environment, which often leads to fear, insecurity, trepidation, and timidity. People may shrivel up or close down in a too critical atmosphere, yet everyone can flourish in an atmosphere of encouragement. For example, you and your helpers should strive to find ways to affirm each participant each week.

There are many ways to encourage participants, especially those who are unrelated to your congregation. A key way of encouragement is for you to begin to know each person well. Start by learning all the participants' names. Write down everyone's name at the first session, pray for the people by name each day during the week, and call each person by name during the second session. Throughout the program, smile at people and express warmth and responsiveness to every participant, especially to those who are not members of your congregation.

Encouragement also involves the gift of engaging others in conversation. Especially try to foster contributions from the quieter members of your group. If one person has done a lot of talking, ask, "What do the rest of you think?" In addition, ask simple, open-ended questions, such as, "What do you think?" and "How do you feel?" and "What has been your experience?" Instead of asking questions that can be answered with either a "Yes" or "No," ask questions that provoke discussion, such as, "How does this story match your experiences?" As a small-group leader you typically should not answer your own questions; if people seem reluctant to answer, try rephrasing. If someone asks you a question that you cannot answer, be honest and say, "I don't know, but I will try to find out by next week."

Remember that all contributions by each member in your small group have value. Even when a group member says something that may appear wrong or silly, positive ways of responding might include, "How interesting!" or "That's a new idea I've never considered!" Create an environment in which your group members can say what they think without fear of embarrassment or ridicule. Involving everyone means taking seriously the ideas, opinions, and insights of each person.

Involvement, however, does not always require speaking. Some people actively participate simply by listening. Grant every person in your group the right to be silent or to say, "Pass" when a question is asked. Silence can be golden. Do not insist that introverts become extroverts. All of these techniques will result in a group whose members understand you as an encourager.

5. Listen. The Letter of James states, "Be quick to listen, slow to speak" (James 1:19). In your small group, speak softly and listen intently. If participants have ideas that are odd or strange, do not respond too quickly (as if their ideas are not even worth considering) or correct them. First, listen. Then try to understand these persons' perspectives or feelings. Finally, show respect. Because listening is more important than speaking, you should not force your own ideas on the group. If someone directly asks you for your own view, answer briefly and then redirect the question to other participants.

6. Keep confidentiality. Assure the members of your small group that their personal stories or issues stay within the group. While your small group may not be bound by rules regarding pastoral confidentiality, gossip and inappropriate conversation outside the group will destroy relationships that are forming. At your first session, insist that people listen carefully to one another and then keep in confidence what is shared in the group. If you perceive that a participant has a particular need or is involved in a crisis, you may wish to share this concern in general with your pastor in a way that does not break confidence.

7. Be a peacemaker. Be gracious, and avoid getting into arguments. Encourage everyone to follow the old Southern saying, "You do not have to like anyone, but you must be courteous to everyone." People rarely change their mind after they get involved in an argument, especially if the disagreement is about religion. It is easy to win an argument and lose a person. If an argument begins, quickly reconcile differences or acknowledge that there are different legitimate opinions. Tears, fears, and anger may all be part of this process; but neither you nor anyone else should dictate how other people respond. Truth is important, but speak the truth in love.

These seven positive qualities—patience, caring, building, encouraging, listening, keeping confidences, and peacemaking—will ensure your success as a small-group leader. When you exhibit these qualities, the way will be smooth.

There are a number of leadership skills that you will also use:

1. Be prepared. If you are not properly prepared, your discussion will flounder. Each week, review the material to be presented; read the appropriate chapter in *Beginnings: Along the Way: A Participant's Companion*; answer the questions for yourself; evaluate your own leadership the previous week; consider each participant and his or her own needs and expectations; and then be ready to lead.

2. Guide the conversation gently. For example, if a participant becomes too dominant, be willing, for the sake of the whole group, to intervene gently by saying, "What do others of you think?" or speak with the person after adjournment. Permitting one participant to dominate, for the sake of avoiding conflict, can have a harmful effect on your discussion. On the opposite side, if you are an excessively dominant leader, you may kill dialogue by doing all the talking instead of giving the participants the freedom to speak and to say what is on their mind. Do not see yourself as an expert with an appropriate response to whatever anyone says; that is, do not dominate the conversation. Silence is okay. In general, if you speak for more than five minutes of the discussion, you have spoken too much. Patience and listening are the needed skills.

3. Avoid fixing individual problems. When someone presents a specific problem to your group, it is tempting for you and others in the group to want to find a solution and fix the problem. Problem solving can make you and other people feel better, wiser, and more powerful; but fixing is not helping. Instead, share your own experiences and let the participants find their own solutions. Also, avoid attempting to convince everyone to follow someone else's personal path. It is far more useful to be able to clarify and celebrate someone else's experience than to urge another person to try to duplicate another's unique experience.

4. Keep a sense of time. Watch the clock, and keep to the schedule. Keep your discussion to the set time. Also, make sure that your group does not spend too much time on a minor question and, as a result, have less time to spend on deeper questions that you know will arise later in the session. Finally, the session should not extend beyond the adjournment time, even if the group members are involved in a lively discussion. It is better to say, "Let's continue this next week," which encourages people to return to continue the dialogue. The danger in going beyond the adjournment time is that some people may hesitate to come back, fearing another late adjournment. If persons wish to stay and continue the conversation, however, you and your helpers should make yourselves available until each participant is ready to leave.

5. Finally, the greatest gift you must have is the gift of prayer. Pray for your small group and for each participant every day. Begin this pattern at the end of your first discussion in the first week by closing the session with prayer. As the small-group leader, take the lead in this prayer, especially in the first few weeks. Your prayers should be brief. If you offer long, poetic prayers, this may hinder other people in the group from offering their own tentative prayers.

As the weeks pass, you may want to invite other members of your group to pray; but be careful not to put anyone on the spot. If you ask participants to pray, instead of asking them spontaneously in front of everyone else, ask them prior to the session so they will have a chance to prepare. If persons are not experienced in praying in public, you may suggest a simple prayer, such as, "Will you ask God to watch over us this next week?" Because many people find praying out loud very difficult, you may wish to introduce a simple prayer model, such as, "Almighty God, (a short petition for each person in your group). We pray in Jesus' name. Amen." Be sensitive to people's feelings, and do not pressure anyone to pray aloud who does not want to do so.

In conclusion, as a small-group leader you need, and God will provide for you, a host of spiritual gifts and leadership skills. When you truly care for the participants and welcome all of them into your community through all your words and actions, God will change lives. Even more so, you who have befriended these persons will also be blessed by God.

SMALL-GROUP HELPERS

In your small discussion group, you may also have one-to-three helpers, hopefully a mix of women and men. Your helpers need to have the same spiritual qualities and gifts as you, although they may be relatively new followers of the Way. Your helpers may even be former participants who just finished a previous program of *Beginnings.*

One of your helpers may be a small-group leader in training or an assistant discussion leader. Serving as a helper is the best way for a person to receive training to be a small-group leader or to serve in some other position the next time the program is offered. There may be occasions when you must miss a session or need special help to bring a discussion back to focus. There may also be times when a group member needs some extra help. This job may be a task you assign to your primary assistant.

If you must miss a session, ask one of your helpers, a person whom the other members know and trust, to lead that session. Ideally, meet with your helper and supply a copy of all the appropriate material. Go over the general outline of the presentation and the discussion questions. Draw on any particular knowledge you have about any of the participants that may be helpful but does not violate confidentiality. Give special attention to preparation details, such as set-up and the closing prayer.

Helpers must understand, however, that their role is to help, not to lead or to dominate. Helpers, sometimes because of their own experiences, may wish to use your small group as a sounding board. Most of the conversation, however, must come from the guest participants, not from the small-group leaders and helpers. Assist your helpers in resisting the temptation to speak first or to speak often. Certainly encourage them not to talk for more than about five minutes of the total discussion time.

SUMMARY

Your small group, the heart of *Beginnings*, brings inquirers into relationship with one another; with your congregation as a whole; and, most importantly, with Jesus Christ. Your leadership of your small group may well serve as the catalyst to fundamental Christian formation for these persons. May God bless your work.

3.
Helping Inquirers Follow Jesus Christ

When you fulfill your role as a small-group leader and the Spirit of God is involved in the process, there is the possibility that participants in your small group may seriously consider redirecting their life toward Jesus Christ. This is the ultimate goal of the program, and you will learn more about this in the first training session. What you will discover is that the most satisfying and terrifying moment for any leader and host of *Beginnings: An Introduction to Christian Faith* is when a participant asks, "How can I become a Christian? How can I follow Jesus?" When a participant asks such questions, you have the opportunity to witness a new birth in Christ. These opportunities will come when you have trusting relationships with participants. When you express a clear, non-manipulative interest in a participant, not as a number but as a person, the conversation will get more serious. The participants watch you every week—what you say, how you act, and where your loyalties lie. When participants see in you a lifestyle that is attractive, they will want to live that way themselves. Participants who find your walk with Jesus Christ intriguing and compelling will want to go further. As your dialogue continues, you must be willing to assist them in understanding Jesus Christ as the true guide. When participants have this experience, we believe that Jesus Christ through the Holy Spirit is inviting them to redirect their lives. Jesus Christ is always knocking on the door of our hearts. Your goal is to help participants hear the knock and discern God's call in their lives.

There are numerous biblical models of spiritual guides helping people hear God's voice and find the gospel feast. Jesus meeting the Samaritan woman at the well in John 4 is a story that can shape how we Christians may share the good news of Jesus Christ with others. We talk about this story in our second session. In this biblical story, Jesus met the woman where she was in her everyday life, drawing water from a well. Jesus paid particular attention to her as an individual, even though a Jewish man speaking to a Samaritan woman was contrary to popular custom. Jesus asked her for a drink of water, thus beginning a conversation with her about something much deeper: water that would quench her thirst forever. Through this conversation, the woman learned that Jesus was indeed the Messiah and could give her living water. This model of sharing the feast—meeting people where they are, caring for them as an individual, beginning a conversation, talking about deep subjects, challenging assumptions, and offering living water—is a wonderful illustration of how you may offer Jesus Christ to your participants.

Another biblical model comes from the disciple Philip in Acts 8. *Beginnings* uses this illustration as the foundation for the sixth session, which is about the Bible. Philip, one of the twelve disciples, was caught up in the activity of the post-Pentecost church in Jerusalem. Then, suddenly, the Holy Spirit led Philip away from his comfort zone to a wilderness road. Philip was willing to go where God wanted him to go. On this road, Philip discovered an inquirer, an Ethiopian official who was already reading God's holy word from the Book of Isaiah. The literal and spiritual journey of the Ethiopian had clearly already begun before Philip's arrival on the scene. Philip simply appeared, felt confident enough to introduce himself to this official, and was knowledgeable enough to answer his questions. But more than just answering questions, Philip was prepared to tell the story of Jesus. Philip clearly knew the Scriptures and was willing to share his journey with Jesus. When the Ethiopian asked for more, Philip provided more. And when the Ethiopian came to a point of decision, Philip was even willing to baptize him in the wilderness. You, also, when you are willing to go into new places, meet new people, discuss challenging questions, and share your experiences with Jesus Christ may point women and men toward the Savior.

We believe that you can be like Jesus and Philip and lead people to living water. At the end of Chapter 7 in the book *Beginnings: Along the Way: A Participant's Companion,* we also describe a few basic steps that are part of making a decision for Jesus Christ. This chapter, especially at its conclusion, offers participants an opportunity to respond to the gift of life Jesus Christ offers. Study this material and other ways to help you share your faith and help lead your participants to Jesus Christ. The following is an excerpt from the material at the end of Chapter 7:

HOW CAN I BEGIN AN INTENTIONAL JOURNEY WITH JESUS CHRIST?
How Can I Become a Christian?

Being a Christian means following Jesus Christ. How does that happen? Do you remember the inquirer in our first session, Nicodemus? Nicodemus was a good man who was looking for the meaning of life. Nicodemus probably fasted twice a week, prayed in the Temple in Jerusalem, gave his money away generously, and even taught religion at the religious academy. Yet with all these good deeds, he was still looking for direction in his journey. Jesus said to Nicodemus, "You must be born from above" (John 3:7).

Because from the moment of birth all human beings are on a spiritual journey, the question is not, "When will you begin your walk with Jesus Christ?" Jesus Christ has always been walking beside you. Rather, the major question is, "Are you ready to begin an intentional, deliberate, and disciplined journey with Jesus Christ?" You have to choose which road to travel. Christians are the people who choose to walk along the way with Jesus Christ. How do you decide? How can you begin?

For each person, the answer is different. In the New Testament and throughout history, each of Jesus' followers came to him differently. Stories of redirection toward Jesus often have more differences than similarities. There is no simple formula, no cookie cutter recipe, no one road map, and no magic words. But all Christians have made a choice to follow Jesus Christ.

Can you choose to follow Jesus Christ today? Of course you can. Should you choose today? That is for you to decide. But if you want to walk down Jesus' path, one way to go is simply to say several very simple words to Jesus Christ. They begin as follows:

1. "Thank you, God," for your love. Jesus said to Nicodemus, "God so loved the world that God gave God's only Son, so that everyone who believes in Jesus Christ may not perish but may have eternal life" (John 3:16; author's translation). You too have to acknowledge God as your loving

Parent. Open your eyes, ears, and heart to see Jesus Christ coming to you and embracing you.

2. "I'm sorry" that I have not been following your way. Jesus began his ministry by telling everyone, "Turn around and believe in the good news" (Mark 1:15; author's translation). If you have been walking down another road, you must admit that you have not been walking with Jesus Christ.

3. "Redirect me," and help me follow Jesus Christ in every step I take. As Peter, another New Testament writer said, "Follow in his [Jesus'] steps" (1 Peter 2:21) and "For you were going astray like sheep, but now you have returned to the shepherds" (1 Peter 2:25). Say to Jesus Christ, "Jesus, be my companion and guide; point me in the right direction."

4. "Let's start" the journey today. As Paul said to some early Christians, "Now is the day of salvation" (2 Corinthians 6:2). Jesus Christ can become your guide today. "If you confess with your lips that Jesus is Lord and believe in your heart that God raised him [Jesus] from the dead, you will be saved" (Romans 10:9). You may choose a new road to travel right now.

It is that simple.

These four phrases—Thank you, I'm sorry, redirect me, let's start—may take the form of a private conversation with God, such as,

"O loving God, I'm sorry about the roads I have traveled. I want to travel with Jesus today. Amen."

or

"Almighty God, I've made some wrong turns and am far from where I need to be. Jesus, guide me now. Amen."

or

"Jesus, I'm sorry. Why don't you take over now? Amen."

These four steps may also take place during a conversation with a Christian friend or another participant in or leader of *Beginnings*. There are people around you in this program who would love to talk with you about following Jesus Christ. Just ask someone you trust.

Meeting Jesus Christ requires making room for him in your life and claiming him as your Guide and Shepherd along the way. Jesus Christ always comes to you. The appropriate response at each moment is to go to him. Despite your doubts, your fears, your denials, you simply have to say "Yes" to Jesus Christ. This new relationship depends on your listening, repenting, and trusting and on being empowered by Jesus Christ. As Jesus told his disciples, "I do not call you servants . . . but I have called you friends" (John 15:15).

For some further reading about how to assist people in their journey, see *The Faith-Sharing New Testament With the Psalms,* by Eddie Fox and George Morris (Cokesbury in cooperation with Thomas Nelson, 1994). This book provides some additional resources about how to be a faithful companion to people considering becoming intentional Christians. Being a spiritual guide for a new birth is one of the highest privileges of being a follower of Jesus Christ. As a leadership team member you must not back away from such an opportunity but claim it as a gift from God.

4.
Training Session 1:
Introduction to *Beginnings*

Your director will conduct the two training sessions for *Beginnings: An Introduction to Christian Faith.* It is vital for you to participate in these sessions. These training sessions are usually held during the two weeks prior to the beginning of the program on the same day and hours that the program will be conducted. If you have a small leadership group, all of this training may take place in one extended session.

The following topics are discussed in the first training session: the nature of this program, the people we are trying to reach, and our motivation in sharing this ministry. You may follow your director's presentation using this resource.

BEGINNINGS: THE PROGRAM

"Evangelism is witness. It is one beggar telling another beggar where to get food. Christians do not offer out of their bounty. They have no bounty. They are simply guests at their Master's table and, as evangelists, they call others too."[1] *Beginnings: An Introduction to Christian Faith* enables you and your fellow leadership team members to share an opening course of the gospel feast with persons seeking God.

We believe that *Beginnings* is one of the most significant programs in which you may ever participate. Why? We believe this because through this program you invite women and men in your community into a living relationship with Jesus Christ by sharing the basic beliefs of our Christian faith from within your congregation. Through this program you and your team are enabled to help fulfill the Great Commission given to us by Jesus: "Go therefore and make disciples of all nations, baptizing them in the name of the Father and of the Son and of the Holy Spirit, and teaching them to obey everything that I have commanded you" (Matthew 28:19-20a).

Beginnings: An Introduction to Christian Faith has a number of distinctive characteristics:

1. Everyone is welcome.

2. Our program is direct and clear.

3. The Bible is our core resource.

4. Our theology is consistent with mainline, Protestant Christianity.

5. Our style is one of gracious invitation.

6. Our illustrations are diverse, and our language is inclusive.

7. Our program is simple.

8. We emphasize your congregational setting.

9. We appeal to persons' hearts and heads.

10. Our program fits the lifestyles of newcomers and new generations.

INQUIRERS: THE AUDIENCE

In *Beginnings* you invite participants into a living relationship with Jesus Christ by sharing the basic beliefs of the Christian faith. Who are these persons? They are the men and women who live next door, work in an adjoining office, eat lunch with you, play on your softball team, exercise with you at the gym, bring their children to your child's birthday party, serve with you on a community board, participate in your supper club, manage your favorite restaurant, come to worship on Christmas Eve, and are part of your extended family. People searching for God, and the people for whom God is searching, are all around us. In the broadest sense, every one of us is an inquirer.

The *Beginnings* program, however, focuses on four primary groups of inquirers (all of whom live in North America and are between twenty-five and forty-five years of age): seekers, cultural Christians, new believers, and new members of your congregation. Seekers and cultural Christians are those men and women who are not a part of an established Christian or other faith community and yet are on a profound spiritual journey. Seekers know very little about Jesus Christ and have never participated in a Christian community. Cultural Christians are people who know a little about Jesus but have a marginal relationship with a congregation. New Christian believers and new members of your congregation are beginning their Christian journey and need additional information for their walk. New believers have experienced a new relationship with Jesus Christ and are just starting an intentional journey with him. New congregational members are the believers in Jesus Christ who have publicly committed to live out their faith in your local community of faith but have not yet become established in your congregation. These four groups are our primary audience.

What about your established congregation members? *Beginnings* encourages them to invite their friends, neighbors, coworkers, and families to come to a meal, share friendly conversation, listen and watch a video/DVD, and discuss their questions. Accompanied by members of the congregation, these persons will begin to know Jesus Christ and recognize the role of God in their life; and they will then want to tell their friends, family members, and coworkers. These friends of congregation members, once they have experienced *Beginnings*, will in turn invite their friends, family members, and coworkers to a subsequent program. Like a stone thrown into a pond, the circle of influence will grow.

REDIRECTION: THE GOAL

Our goal in *Beginnings* is to redirect people toward the way of Jesus Christ. Through the power of the Holy Spirit, your congregation may utilize this program to point women and men toward a deep, lifelong relationship with Jesus Christ. *Beginnings* is evangelistic in the best sense of the word: sharing the first tastes of the gospel feast with inquirers seeking God.

"Redirection" is our word for the first steps toward conversion. Conversion is God's gift of grace that enables persons to turn from one set of relationships to another. Because we believe that such a "turning to Jesus

Christ" encompasses the whole of a person's life, we do not expect anyone to be converted (in the fullest sense) simply by participating in *Beginnings*. Yet, this program gives women and men the opportunity to make a conscious choice to begin going in a new direction that may ultimately lead to a life-long commitment to Jesus Christ. In other words, our goal is to open up the way that leads to conversion. This means you should not feel pressure to "produce" tangible results from this program. What occurs from the shared experience of this program is primarily a work of the Holy Spirit.

This process is holistic. This redirection involves both the heart and the mind of participants. For this reason, *Beginnings* strives for intellectual integrity. As a Bible story is presented each week and Christian beliefs are explained, inquirers are equipped with the tools to make a rational decision for or against Christianity. Redirection toward Jesus Christ includes not only rational consent but also trust, however. The gospel calls women and men to fall in love with Jesus Christ. For this reason, *Beginnings* also speaks the language of the heart. Christian beliefs and practices are discussed in response to the real life questions of participants. By appealing to both the head and the heart, *Beginnings* encourages participants to begin the lifelong journey of responding to the invitation of Jesus Christ, a journey that will demand their whole self.

Helping persons come into a living relationship with Jesus Christ in your community of faith does not happen overnight but comes by taking a number of initial steps along the way. As people participate in this program, we believe that all of the following initial steps are possible:

1. They may acknowledge or have awakened in them a hunger for Jesus Christ.

2. They may begin to understand the relevance of Christianity to modern life.

3. They may practice briefly some of the basic ways Christians experience God: fellowship with other Christians, Bible study, Christian testimonies, and prayer.

4. They may make a commitment to Jesus Christ and begin an intentional spiritual journey.

5. They may consider church membership.

As persons participate in *Beginnings*, each of these steps is possible, though none is required. They are merely markers in a potential journey of Christian discipleship.

As your congregation shares in the mission of evangelism, new persons are invited into a relationship with Jesus Christ; and the church fulfills its commission.

1. From "Venite Adoremus II," in *World's Student Christian Federation Prayer Book*; pages 105ff.

5.
Training Session 2:
Preparing for *Beginnings*

The second training session focuses on the practical details that will enable this program to succeed. You may follow your director's presentation using this book. In this training session we discuss the various resources used in this program, its key elements, basic housekeeping details that involve your participation, the tasks of various team members, and an outline of a typical session.

BASIC RESOURCES

There are five basic resources for *Beginnings: An Introduction to Christian Faith*:

Beginnings: Director's Manual provides the theological background to the program and basic information needed to use *Beginnings* in your congregation. Your director will use this resource.

Beginnings: Video Resources is a series of twelve presentations by Rob Weber (each approximately fifteen-minutes long) about the basics of Christianity.

Beginnings: Small-Group Leader's Guide guides your small-group discussions following the video presentation.

Beginnings: Participant's Guide is the participants' workbook. Each participant has one of these books.

Beginnings: Along the Way: A Participant's Companion is an engaging book that parallels and complements the video resource. This book provides the core biblical story, additional scriptural references, and supplemental illustrations that were the basis of and expand upon the basic presentations. *Along the Way* is a helpful companion for you and other participants throughout this journey.

Each participant also needs a Bible throughout the program. We recommend either the New Revised Standard Version or the New International Version.

KEY CHARACTERISTICS

Beginnings has a number of key characteristics that are part of each session. Each of the following foundational elements is essential to everyone's positive experience of the program:

1. Inviting

2. Eating

3. Laughing

4. Singing and Worshiping

5. Learning

6. Asking

7. Sharing

HOUSEKEEPING DETAILS

At your first group session, your director will provide you with a blank "Contact Sheet" on which to write the following information: name of participant, telephone number, and e-mail address. Understand, however, that this contact information is being collected only for special needs, such as the necessity to inform participants that a session has been canceled or to alert persons about a problem. Turn in your "Contact Sheet" to your director at the end of the first session; your director will make a copy and return the original to you as soon as possible. Do not give each member of your small group or anyone else a copy of the "Contact Sheet." If participants want to exchange addresses and telephone numbers, they may do this individually. If anyone asks you for this information, do not/share it under any circumstances. Respect and honor the participants' privacy.

Toward the end of the program, your director will give each participant a "Participant Questionnaire." The information participants provide will help your team evaluate the program and leaders and assist you in planning the next program.

Your director will also give you your own "Small-Group Leader's Questionnaire" about your experience with the program. The form asks you which group members completed the program and if a person did not complete it, why (if you know). Also, we will ask you to describe briefly how your group members are going to continue their spiritual journey and who could give a good witness to God's work in their life at the final Love Feast. Finally, we will ask which participants might serve as helpers during a future program.

Please take these forms seriously and prepare them promptly.

YOUR TEAM

The *Beginnings* leadership team consists of the servant guides who will be the enablers of the program in your congregation. That is, you and the other members of your team are the companions for inquirers on the way; you are the midwives who make new birth in Jesus Christ possible in the birthing room of your congregation. When conducting this program, you and the other guides may have only one task; or you may have multiple assignments. Your team members are the hands, feet, ears, and mouths of the body of Christ, who make visible to all the participants Jesus Christ himself.

The following persons will manage the various tasks necessary for the program: pastor, director, music/worship leader, meal coordinator, treasurer, you and the other small-group discussion leaders, and small-group helpers.

In programs with a small number of participants, not every task or assignment needs a different person; as few as two people can lead a program for eight other people. The goal is to have the right number of team members so that everyone has a significant role to play but no team member is overwhelmed by her or his responsibilities.

As many as one-third of the participants in the program may be leaders and helpers from your host congregation. This many congregational hosts are needed in order to have at least three members from your congregation in each small group. All of your team members need to have an active faith in Jesus Christ. They must be gracious to guests, familiar with Scripture, comfortable with small groups, and attentive to the movement of the Spirit in a group.

Throughout *Beginnings*, you and all the team members will work hard and must have a high level of commitment. Participants will only reach the level of commitment exhibited by everyone on your team. If every member of your leadership team does not attend each session, the participants will be unlikely to do so. Make the serious effort to do the necessary preparation, to attend all the sessions, to talk with participants instead of friends in the congregation, and to concentrate on the task. Occasions will arise when you are unable to attend a session, but this program must be a high priority in your life.

Your pastor, the shepherd of the people of God, is the key to the success of *Beginnings* in your church. As the spiritual guide of a congregation, she or he needs to demonstrate strong, visible, and vocal support of the program, possibly even serving as your director. Please listen to and follow the leadership of your pastor.

Your director must have the gifts of organization and leadership, as well as the ability to speak well in front of a group of inquirers. He or she has a number of specific responsibilities and may well ask you to assist in a number of ways. Please help in every way requested.

Your music/worship leader (not all programs will include music) uses his or her gift of music to touch people's emotions, proclaim the faith, and point women and men toward God. This ministry may be rather large in your group, or it may be fairly limited. If there is singing, however, please be an enthusiastic singer. All of the participants will take their cue from you and others on your team.

Your meal coordinator is responsible for the food and all the related activities. Some of your small-group helpers may be recruited to assist in the preparation and serving of the meal. Even if you do not like the food served, thank the meal coordinator after each meal.

Your treasurer keeps all the financial accounts, makes necessary purchases, and assists other team members in purchasing the supplies they need. We suggest that it is best not to charge participants who are not members of your host congregation for the program as a whole or for the various parts of the program, such as the weekly meal and materials. You, however, as a congregational host, may be asked to contribute to the meal each week.

Everyone's commitment is for two training sessions, twelve small-group sessions, and follow-up after the program to welcome and possibly incorporate participants into your congregation. Even if you have helped with several *Beginnings* programs or feel that you are an expert in small groups, you should still come to the two training sessions every time the program is offered.

Also essential for everyone is a commitment to the program in prayer. Pray regularly for every aspect of *Beginnings*: your team as a whole, the meal, the video/DVD presentations, and the individual members of your team. Also commit yourself to pray for every participant in your small group.

Remember, the success of *Beginnings* depends on your team members, who guide each program. When they reach out to their friends, neighbors, family members, coworkers, and other inquirers, God will give them the skills they need to share the Lord's banquet with everyone.

Finally, be assured that your program will be successful, not because of the skills of your team members, but because of God's grace. God alone inspires your leaders, the Holy Spirit empowers your team, and the destination is clearly God's kingdom.

THE WEEKLY SESSIONS

Beginnings may be held in the morning, at midday, or in the evening. Your director will share the schedule with you, both for each week and for the whole program. Each program, however, has the following pattern of activities:

At the beginning, before any participants arrive, all your team members gather for a few minutes for organization and prayer. During this time your director guides a brief discussion about the theme of the session and any necessary housekeeping details. You can assist by mentioning other details necessary for the session to go well. This preparation time ends with prayer led by your director. This orientation meeting concludes before the participants begin to arrive so that your team members may go out and welcome the gathering participants. Your task is to go to your table and greet participants when they come to eat with you.

There is a meal. Eating together, especially as a small group, is an essential part of the program. Typically, your small discussion group sits together; and you and your helpers act as hosts and facilitate the conversations. During the meal, there should be no agenda other than encouraging people to visit with one another in a relaxed way. The goal of the meal is for participants to become friends with one another.

Your director now welcomes everyone briefly and describes the focus of the session.

Your music/worship leader may choose to have a brief time of music.

The video/DVD presentation offers the content of the session. Using *Beginnings: Video Resources* encourages everyone to follow along in *Beginnings: Participant's Guide*. The participant's guide contains the biblical text for the session, room for notes about the presentation, and some leading questions. There is also space for people to jot down some notes that they may use during the discussion that follows.

Finally, your director invites everyone to break into the assigned small groups. Your task now begins in earnest. Use the gifts and skills we discussed in Chapter 2.

At the end of your discussion, close the conversation and end with prayer. Dismiss people from your small group without returning to the larger group. At this point, the session is over and people may leave. Some persons will wish to remain and talk together, but no participant should be forced to stay beyond the announced ending time. All your leaders are to remain until all the participants have left. Then gather for a few moments to make plans for the next session.

Part Two:

Leading *Beginnings* Session Outlines for Small-Group Leaders

Session 1:
So, Is This All There Is?

Introduction

All people are searching for meaning in their lives. We wonder why we are here, what our purpose is, where we can find guidance. Followers of Jesus believe that in our spiritual journey, Christ is the one who provides a solution to the problem of the restlessness in our lives and accompanies us on our journey. We invite you to join us in the journey to find answers to our most important questions.

PREPARATION

Prepare yourself spiritually. Pray for yourself and for all the participants. Review these small-group leader's notes.

Read Chapter 1 in *Beginnings: Along the Way: A Participant's Companion.*

Prepare the area where your small group will meet. Put out pencils/pens, and place Bibles under one chair or on a side table.

OPENING HOSPITALITY

Do not greet participants at the door. Stay at your assigned meal table to greet members of your small group, and introduce your small-group members to one another.

Ask participants to introduce themselves to persons at your table by telling one important thing about themselves that no one at the table knows.

SERVE THE MEAL

WELCOME *(5 minutes by director)*

SINGING *(5 minutes by music/worship leader)*

VIDEO/DVD PRESENTATION 1 *(20 minutes)*

DISCUSSION *(45 minutes by small-group leader)*

Prepare the chairs for small-group discussion. Put out pencils/pens, and place all the Bibles under one chair or on a side table if you have not already done so.

Pass around the contact form for the first time. Remind participants that this information will be used only under special circumstances.

Speak about the issue of confidentiality. Remind everyone that what is shared in the small group should stay in the small group.

Group Questions

If your house were burning down and all your family and pets were safe and you only had time to save one item (no matter how difficult it would be to move it), what would you save? Why?

A lot of people sum up their basic approach to life on the bumper stickers they place on their cars:

"Normal People Worry Me"
"My Karma Ran Over Your Dogma"
"Money Isn't Everything . . . But It Sure Keeps the Kids in Touch"
"Compost Happens"
"It's as Bad as You Think and They Are Out to Get You"

If you were to create your own bumper sticker, what would it say? How would it reflect your philosophy of life?

Rob described one of his earliest disappointments in life, the time he ordered "sea monkeys" from the back page of a comic book. Can you remember a time as a child when you were really excited about something—a toy, an event, or an experience—only to wonder later, "So, is this all there is?" Can you recall a more recent experience that made you ask this same question? If so, what happened?

Did you hear anything else from Rob that connects with your life? If so, what?

Personal Questions

Can you identify with Nicodemus looking for Jesus at night? Why or why not? What would his friends have said if they had known he had gone to visit with Jesus?

What would your family and friends say if they knew you were participating in *Beginnings*?

Do you believe that this is all there is? Is your heart satisfied or restless with the answers you've come up with so far?

What do you hope to learn through participating in *Beginnings*?

Can you remember a significant time of yearning to experience God? If so, where were you? How did you respond? Did you try to forget it? Did you feel unnerved? Did you embrace the yearning? Do you now have a yearning to know more about God?

CLOSING *(5 minutes by small-group leader)*

Remind everyone about the schedule for next week, and make other necessary announcements.

Pass around the contact form again. Remind participants this information will be used only under special circumstances.

Invite the participants to pause for a minute of silence to reflect on this session.

Pray together.

Adjourn on time.

SPECIAL NOTE

After the participants have left, meet with the members of your leadership team briefly to review the first session and to identify any corrections you need to make for the next session. Turn in the "Contact Sheet" to your director.

Session 2:
Who Is Jesus, and Why Should I Care?

Jesus Christ

INTRODUCTION

Through the story of the woman at the well, we discover that in the midst of our searching, God through Jesus Christ is searching for us.

PREPARATION

Prepare yourself spiritually. Pray for yourself and for all the participants.
Review these small-group leader's notes.
Read Chapter 2 in *Beginnings: Along the Way: A Participant's Guide.*
Prepare the area where the small group will meet.

OPENING HOSPITALITY

Welcome all participants.
Ask people to introduce themselves further at your table to other persons in their small group.

SERVE THE MEAL

WELCOME *(5 minutes by director)*

SINGING *(5 minutes by music/worship leader)*

VIDEO/DVD PRESENTATION 2 *(20 minutes)*

DISCUSSION *(45 minutes by small-group leader)*

Greet each member of your small group.

Pass around the contact form for the last time; it will be used only under special circumstances. At the end of the session, give it to the director.

Remind everyone about confidentiality. What is said within the small group should stay within the small group.

Group Questions

When you were a child, how did you answer the question, "What do you want to be when you grow up?" How accurate was your prediction?

Who do you think Jesus is? What names or titles do you use for Jesus: teacher, healer, social activist, magician, messiah, religious fanatic, mystic, hopeless romantic, enlightenment philosopher, hoax, compassionate friend, martyr? Why?

Imagine you are sitting on a park bench and Jesus comes and sits beside you. What would you do?

_____ Keep reading the paper and hope he does not notice you.
_____ Try to strike up a conversation. What would your opening line be?
_____ Run.
_____ Ask for a favor. What would you ask for?
_____ Ask his advice. What would you want to know?
_____ What reaction would you expect from Jesus?

Take a moment and pair up with another person in your group. Ask each other: "What brings you to the well?"

Personal Questions

Can you see yourself as the woman at the well, looking for water and being found by Jesus? How do you think the people in her town responded when she told them about her conversation with Jesus?

What are you seeking?

CLOSING (5 minutes by small-group leader)

Remind everyone about the schedule for next week, and make other necessary announcements.

Invite the participants to pause for a minute of silence to reflect on this session.

Pray together.

Adjourn on time.

Session 3:
Why Am I Not Where
I Want to Be?

Sin and the Cross

INTRODUCTION

Through the tax collector Zacchaeus, we discover that when our lives seem to be falling apart, Jesus comes to us.

PREPARATION

Prepare yourself spiritually. Pray for yourself and for all the participants.
Review these small-group leader's notes.
Read Chapter 3 in *Beginnings: Along the Way: A Participant's Guide*.
Prepare the area where your small group will meet.

The pattern each week will include the meal, the welcome, singing, and the video/DVD presentation.

DISCUSSION *(45 minutes by small-group leader)*

Greet each member of your small group.

Group Questions

Have you ever had an experience like Rob's in which you felt in over your head or overwhelmed?
What are your top two choices in describing human nature?

____ selfish
____ good
____ naïve

___ evil
___ generous
___ innocent
___ clueless
___ other

Why did you make those choices?

Take a moment and pair up with another person in your group (different from the person you paired up with last week), and ask each other: "Where do you want to be? Why are you not there? How do you get there?"

Personal Questions

Can you identify with Zacchaeus watching for Jesus, with the crowd who observed their conversation, or with Jesus' friends who observed them? How do you think people responded when Zacchaeus showed up on their doorstep paying back everything he had stolen?

What are your dreams for your life? What is holding you back from achieving them?

Are you where you want to be in your life? If not, what is really keeping you from being where you want to be in your life?

Describe a situation in which one wrong deed led to another.

CLOSING *(5 minutes by small-group leader)*

Remind everyone about the schedule for next week, and make other necessary announcements.

Invite the participants to pause for a minute of silence to reflect on this session.

Pray together.

Adjourn on time.

Session 4:
What Happens When I Die?

Death and the Resurrection

INTRODUCTION

Through the story of two people on the day after the Crucifixion, we discover that the resurrection of Jesus Christ is God's answer to the problem of death.

PREPARATION

Prepare yourself spiritually. Pray for yourself and for all the participants.
Review these small-group leader's notes.
Read Chapter 4 in *Beginnings: Along the Way: A Participant's Guide.*
Prepare the area where your small group will meet.

DISCUSSION *(45 minutes by small-group leader)*

Greet each member of your small group.

Group Questions

Reporters from a British newspaper frequently ask celebrities, "How would you like to die?" Suppose a reporter has just arrived at your home and has asked you this question. How would you answer?

Name a person close to you who has died. What was your reaction?

Have you had an experience in your life that brought you to the point where you felt like you had been given a second life?

What do you believe happens when you die? In what way, if any, does your response make a difference in the way you live today?

Personal Questions

Recall your answer to the group question about the person close to you who died. What other thoughts or feelings do you have about the death of that person?

Imagine yourself walking along with the couple on the road to Emmaus, or imagine yourself with the friends back in Jerusalem who heard their story. What insights do you gain from them?

If you could write your own obituary, what would you say? What have you accomplished in your life? What has been left undone? If you have time, you may wish to write out your own obituary.

CLOSING *(5 minutes by small-group leader)*

Remind everyone about the schedule for next week, and make other necessary announcements.

Invite the participants to pause for a minute of silence to reflect on this session.

Pray together.

Adjourn on time.

Session 5:
Can I Trust God?

Providence and Suffering

INTRODUCTION

Can we trust God when our lives and world seem to be in chaos? Through the story of Moses, we are reminded that God has a plan that has existed since the beginning of creation for everyone to be in relationship with God.

PREPARATION

Prepare yourself spiritually. Pray for yourself and for all the participants.
Review these small-group leader's notes.
Read Chapter 5 in *Beginnings: Along the Way: A Participant's Guide*.
Prepare the area where the small group will meet.

DISCUSSION *(45 minutes by small-group leader)*

Greet each member of your small group.

Group Questions

Who are the people in your life who influenced your idea of God the most? Was their influence positive or negative? In what ways?
How did you picture God when you were a child?

____ a gentle grandfather with a long white beard or grandmother in a rocking chair
____ a stern judge in a black robe
____ a bored spectator watching from a distance
____ other
____ I never thought about God when I was growing up

How has your view of God changed? In what ways has it remained the same?

When things get really tough, who is the one person you can really trust?

When people say, "Trust God," what is your reaction?

Personal Questions

Moses was startled by a burning bush. Have you ever had such an experience? If so, what were the circumstances? What do you think Moses' wife and family said when he got home and told about his experience?

Have you ever had an experience that made you ask, "Where is God?" If so, what was it?

When have you had an experience when God came up and got right in your face? What was happening in your life both before and after that experience?

Do you find it hard to trust God with the things that are most important to you? Why or why not?

What would your ideal parent look like? What difference would it make in your life if you began to see God this way?

What does it mean to trust God in a world that has experienced the Jewish Holocaust, global terrorism, child abuse, poverty, and children being born with birth defects?

CLOSING *(5 minutes by small-group leader)*

Remind everyone about the schedule for next week, and make other necessary announcements.

Invite the participants to pause for a minute of silence to reflect on this session.

Pray together.

Adjourn on time.

SPECIAL NOTE

Begin to promote the Day Apart retreat and to register people for it if you are using the nine-week model.

Session 6:
How Does God Speak to Me?

The Bible

INTRODUCTION

When an Ethiopian official was looking for answers, he turned to the Scriptures for direction in his relationship with God.

PREPARATION

Prepare yourself spiritually. Pray for yourself and for all the participants.
Review these small-group leader's notes.
Read Chapter 6 in *Beginnings: Along the Way: A Participant's Guide*.
Prepare the area where the small group will meet.

SPECIAL NOTE

Make sure that extra Bibles are available.

DISCUSSION *(45 minutes by small-group leader)*

Greet each member of your small group.

Group Questions

If you own a Bible, when did you receive it?
What has been your experience when reading the Bible? (Check all that apply.)

____ My mind wanders.
____ It's boring.

___ I don't understand the words or context.
___ I discover people like me.
___ I'm intimidated.
___ God speaks to me.

Name some ways other than the Bible in which God speaks.

How do you respond to Rob's descriptions of the Bible as an oracle, charm, rulebook, confirmation of beliefs held, or as a road map or guide?

· What did you hear from Rob that connects with your life?

Personal Questions

The Ethiopian official was looking for answers and needed some help. When have you felt this way? When have you helped someone else in this same situation?

Has God ever spoken to you? If so, how? What did God say?

Have you had an occasion when you read the Bible for instruction, direction, or help? If so, when? Why? What did you discover?

If you have a favorite Bible story, what is it? Why is it important to you?

Read from the New Testament a story when Jesus feed 4,000 people, Mark 8:1-10. Practice interpreting the Bible: What is this story about? How does this story connect with you? What does the story expect from you?

Read also from the New Testament a story about a sower throwing out some seed, Mark 4:1-8. Practice interpreting the Bible: What is this story about? How does this story connect with you? What does the story expect from you? After you have thought about the story, read Mark 4:13-20 for Jesus' interpretation of the story. How does Jesus' interpretation change how you understand the story?

If you are really adventurous, try reading the entire New Testament book of Mark. Doing so takes about one hour and covers the whole of Jesus' life from his baptism in the river Jordan to his resurrection in Jerusalem.

CLOSING *(5 minutes by small-group leader)*

Remind everyone about the schedule for the Day Apart retreat (if you are following the nine-week option) and for next week's session. Also make other necessary announcements.

Continue registering for the Day Apart retreat.

Invite the participants to pause for a minute of silence to reflect on this session.

Pray together.

Adjourn on time.

SPECIAL NOTE

Turn in the Day Apart retreat registration form to your director.

Session 7 (Day Apart 1): If I Don't Feel Lost, Why Do I Need to Be Found?

Salvation and Conversion

INTRODUCTION

Through the story of a runaway son, we hear that God invites each of us on a lifelong journey during which our relationship with God deepens.

PREPARATION

Make sure everyone has a schedule.

Prepare yourself spiritually. Pray for yourself and for all the participants.

If you are doing the Day Apart retreat, review these small-group leader's notes for all three sessions. Also read Chapters 7, 8, and 9 in *Beginnings: Along the Way: A Participant's Companion.* The times of discussion and additional notes all refer to the Day Apart retreat model.

If you are not doing the Day Apart retreat, continue your usual pattern of reading one chapter prior to each weekly session and close in the usual way.

DISCUSSION *(50 minutes by small-group leader)*

Greet each member of your small group.

Group Questions

Recall a time when you returned to your hometown or old school or some other place after a long absence. How did it feel? In what ways was it awkward? In what ways was it comforting? Why?

Has there been a time in your life when you felt like the younger son or like the waiting father or like the older brother who stayed behind? If so, what were the circumstances? Why did you feel that way?

Has anyone ever approached you about God in a way that turned you off? On the other hand, have you ever had an experience that ignited a spark to seek God more earnestly? If so, what was it?

At this point in your spiritual journey, where are you in your relationship with God?

Personal Questions

Take some time for the following exercise: Draw a chart of your own personal spiritual journey. Use a single line that represents your relationship to God. At each valley, peak, gentle hill, or plateau, write down the event, person, or experience that was involved.

Do you feel lost or found or just comfortable in your spiritual journey? Why?

CLOSING [of First Day Apart Retreat Session]
(5 minutes by small-group leader)

Remind everyone about the break and the schedule for the rest of the day (if you are having the Day Apart retreat).

Invite the participants to pause for a minute of silence to reflect on this session.

Pray together.

Adjourn on time.

DAY APART RETREAT SHORT BREAK (10 minutes)

Session 8 (Day Apart 2): Can I Start Again?

Forgiveness and Wholeness

INTRODUCTION

Through two stories we hear that a relationship with Jesus opens for us the possibilities of being forgiven and forgiving other people and finding wholeness in body, mind, spirit, and relationships.

DISCUSSION *(35 minutes by small-group leader)*

Greet each member of your small group.

Group Questions

Have you ever known anyone who changed completely? How or why did it happen? Did you like the person better before or after the change?

Name someone close to you who needs forgiveness in his or her life. Why does this person need forgiveness?

Name someone close to you who needs healing in her or his life. Why does this person need healing?

Can you identify with the biblical woman in trouble or with the crowd ready to stone her or with the bleeding woman? Why or why not?

Personal Questions

What area in your life needs forgiveness?

Is God nudging you to forgive someone or to restore a broken relationship?

What area in your life needs healing?

If you could start your life over from this point on, with no baggage and no past, what would your life look like?

CLOSING *[of Second Day Apart Retreat Session]*
(5 minutes by small-group leader)

Remind everyone about the break and the schedule for the rest of the day (if you are having the Day Apart retreat).

Invite the participants to pause for a minute of silence to reflect on this session.

Pray together.

Adjourn on time.

DAY APART RETREAT SHORT BREAK BEFORE LUNCH
(15 minutes)

DAY APART RETREAT LUNCH AND FREE TIME
(1 hour and 15 minutes)

Session 9 (Day Apart 3): How Do I Speak to God?

Prayer

INTRODUCTION

Jesus teaches us that prayer is speaking and listening to God.

DISCUSSION *(40 minutes by small-group leader)*

Greet each member of your small group.

Group Questions

How often do you speak with your best friend? Is it often enough? What keeps you from talking more often?

Read The Lord's Prayer aloud as a group. What is it saying?

Rob described prayer as "drawing near to God," an experience that can happen through words, wood, or life. Can you name a time when you prayed to God without using any words? If so, what were the circumstances?

If you had the opportunity to talk with God alone and uninterrupted, what would be one of the first things you would say?

Personal Questions

The disciples asked Jesus how to pray. Why do you think they asked Jesus this question?

When you pray, do you think God is listening? Why do you think that?

Have any of your prayers been answered? If so, how?

Have any of your prayers gone unanswered? Do you have any idea why?

Write down some prayer requests for:

yourself
your family
your friends
your community
your nation
our world

Pray for someone you dislike: an ex-spouse, an ex-friend, a former boss, an estranged family member.

Read Matthew 6:5-13. What does Jesus tell us about prayer? What does this message tell you about how to pray? Will you pray any differently having heard this message? Why or why not?

Consider praying The Lord's Prayer each day in the coming week.

CLOSING *[of Third Day Apart Retreat Session]*
(10 minutes by small-group leader)

Remind everyone about the day's final schedule and the schedule for next week. Also make any other necessary announcements.

Begin to promote the Love Feast closing celebration.

See if people are available for supper after the end of the day's sessions (Day Apart model).

Invite the participants to pause for a minute of silence to reflect on this session.

Pray together about the whole day's experience (Day Apart retreat model).

Adjourn on time for a break and (optional) to prepare for Holy Communion (Day Apart retreat model).

SPECIAL NOTE

Begin to advertise for the Love Feast at this time, using the invitations provided by your director.

Session 10:
How Can I Make a Life and Not Just a Living?

The Good Life

INTRODUCTION

Following Jesus Christ demands a different way of living that focuses on loving God and loving other people.

PREPARATION

Prepare yourself spiritually. Pray for yourself and for all the participants. Review these small-group leader's notes.

Read Chapter 10 in *Beginnings: Along the Way: A Participant's Companion.*

Prepare the area where your small group will meet.

SPECIAL NOTE

Get the registration sheets for the Love Feast and the invitations to the Love Feast from your director.

DISCUSSION *(45 minutes by small-group leader)*

Greet each member of your small group.

Group Questions

Divide your small group into two teams. The first team will advocate "the good life" as defined by people in your grandparents' generation. The second team will advocate "the good life" as defined by your own generation. At the end of the debate, discuss which generation is more or less satisfied by their answers.

Who or what is in control of your life now?

____ to-do list
____ your PDA
____ your e-mail inbox
____ your children
____ your employer
____ your 401K or pension plan
____ an ex-friend
____ your career
____ your money and possessions
____ God

How do you respond to Rob's statement, "We are seeking to fill our lives with other things rather than the one thing that was made to fulfill us."

Who has modeled an authentic, joyful life for you? What makes this person special?

Personal Questions

Think about your favorite fantasies as a child. What roles did you play? Someone's hero? Someone's beauty? Having a particular profession? How relevant do these fantasies seem to your life now? If you could adopt a new role for your life, what would it be?

What is the primary thing/commandment/law/goal in your life? Does your primary thing/commandment/law/goal seem consistent with God's commandment/law/goal for you?

What are some qualities that you believe are fundamental to a good life?

Do you make a living, or do you have a life?

CLOSING *(7 minutes by small-group leader)*

Remind everyone about the schedule for next week, and make any other necessary announcements.

Invite the participants to pause for a minute of silence to reflect on this session.

Pray together.

Adjourn on time.

SPECIAL NOTES

Promote the closing Love Feast, especially inviting family and friends to come and participate. Pass around the registration form for the Love Feast and distribute invitations for participants to give to friends.

Tell people that at the next session (11), each participant will be asked to speak about each other participant in the group and to name one gift that person possesses. For example, someone may say, "John has the gift of compassion." or "Susan has the gift of honesty." Ask the participants to think about one another and one another's gifts in the week ahead. If they believe that they will be uncomfortable sharing verbally, they may choose simply to write something down for each person and be ready to hand it to the person next week.

Write down your own affirmation of each person for the next session.

Session 11:
Why Should I Join Any Group That Will Have Me as a Member?

Church Membership

INTRODUCTION

Based on an illustration about the human body, we discover that following Jesus Christ includes being part of a church community.

PREPARATION

Prepare yourself spiritually. Pray for yourself and for all the participants. Review these small-group leader's notes.

Read Chapter 11 in *Beginnings: Along the Way: A Participant's Companion.*

Complete your affirmations about each participant, and write each affirmation on a separate card.

Complete your small-group leader questionnaire, and turn it in to your director.

Prepare the area where your small group will meet.

DISCUSSION *(45 minutes by small-group leader)*

SPECIAL NOTES

Obtain from your director copies of the questionnaires for participants and your own small-group leader questionnaire prior to breaking into small groups. Also pass out registration forms for the Love Feast and invitations to the Love Feast.

Begin this time of sharing by asking each participant to share with the other persons in their group the spiritual gifts they see in one another. This may be done orally or in written form on slips of paper. This is a time to affirm the God-given gifts and fruits of the Spirit that each person has. As the small-group leader you should speak last, to give everyone else the chance to speak first.

Group Questions

Name the part of the human body that best describes you. Why?

Go around the circle and share with one another the gifts you assigned each person (see the end of last week's session for details).

With what group/sports team/ethnic group/hobby/interest do you identify?

When someone says to you, "Let's go to church!" what image or feeling first comes to your mind?

Personal Questions

What is the one place in the world that you would most like to visit? Imagine you have just won four free tickets to go there. Whom would you take with you? Why did you ask these people? What does this choice of this place and these people say about you?

Name the people in your life who have really taken the time to get to know you. How did they show you that they care? Do you have more or fewer of these people in your life as the years go by?

Have you ever been in a church where you felt the presence of God? If so, what was it like?

What would it be like for you to be a part of a community that cares for the outcast?

Can you see yourself as part of such a community? Why or why not?

Having experienced *Beginnings*, are you more likely to give a congregation a chance? Why?

CLOSING *(5 minutes by small-group leader)*

Remind everyone about the schedule for next week, and make other necessary announcements.

Invite the participants to pause for a minute of silence to reflect on this session.

Adjourn on time.

SPECIAL NOTES

Continue to register people for the Love Feast, encouraging family and friends to attend by using the Love Feast invitations. Pass out the invitations. Register people.

Turn in the Love Feast registration form to the meal coordinator.

Pass out the participant questionnaire, and ask participants to fill it out before they leave or by next week.

Take home and fill out your small-group leader questionnaire about each participant in your group. Return it next week.

Session 12:
Love Feast!

Remembering, Sharing, and Continuing the Journey

Personal Questions

How have you experienced God over these past weeks? What has surprised you?

What have you discovered about yourself?

What are you going to do next?

Whom are you going to tell?

What is the biggest decision you are facing at this time in your life? To whom, if anyone, will you look for help in making this decision?

We encourage everyone to remember the experiences they have had during *Beginnings* and to celebrate what each participant has discovered about God.

Your director is in charge of this session. Relax and enjoy.

Be sure to turn in your small-group leader questionnaire to your director.